Monkey Business

RHESUS MONKEYS

Gillian Gosman

PowerKiDS
press™
New York

Published in 2012 by The Rosen Publishing Group, Inc.
29 East 21st Street, New York, NY 10010

First Edition

Editor: Jennifer Way
Book Design: Kate Laczynski

Photo Credits: Cover, pp. 1, 5, 6, 8, 9, 12, 13, 20, 21 Shutterstock.com; p. 4 iStockphoto/Thinkstock; p. 7 (left) Anup Shah/Photodisc/Thinkstock; p. 7 (right) Visuals Unlimited, Inc./Gerald & Buff Corsi/ Getty Images; p. 10 © www.iStockphoto.com/fotoVoyager; p. 11 Anup Shah/Digital Vision/Thinkstock; pp. 14–15, 16 © Tao Images/age fotostock; p. 17 Stele/Getty Images; p. 18 James Warwick/Getty Images; p. 19 Tier Images/Getty Images; p. 22 Christophe Archambault/AFP/Getty Images.

Library of Congress Cataloging-in-Publication Data

Gosman, Gillian.
 Rhesus monkeys / by Gillian Gosman. — 1st ed.
    p. cm. — (Monkey business)
 ISBN 978-1-4488-5023-5 (library binding) — ISBN 978-1-4488-5181-2 (pbk.) —
 ISBN 978-1-4488-5182-9 (6-pack)
 1. Rhesus monkey—Juvenile literature. I. Title. II. Series.
 QL737.P93G676 2012
 599.8'643–dc22

                                                        2011003072

Manufactured in the United States of America

CPSIA Compliance Information: Batch #WS11PK: For Further Information contact Rosen Publishing, New York, New York at 1-800-237-9932

Contents

Meet the Rhesus Monkey.. 4

Macaques 6

An Old World Monkey 8

An Adaptable Monkey.. 10

Time to Eat! 12

Living Together 14

Monkeying Around 16

Males and Females 18

Baby Monkeys 20

A Problem for People 22

Glossary 23

Index.. 24

Web Sites.. 24

MEET THE RHESUS MONKEY

Rhesus monkeys are a **species** within a group of monkeys called macaques. Macaques are one of the world's most widespread monkeys. Rhesus monkeys are the best-known macaques.

There are six subspecies of rhesus monkeys. A subspecies is a smaller grouping within a species.

Rhesus monkeys walk mostly on four limbs. They can walk on their back legs for short distances, though.

As are other monkeys, rhesus monkeys are **primates**. They are very intelligent, **social** animals. Humans are primates, too. Rhesus monkeys are like humans in many ways. In fact, people have studied rhesus monkeys not only to learn more about these animals, but also to make discoveries in medicine and science. This book will introduce you to this interesting monkey.

MACAQUES

The rhesus monkey is one of 22 species of macaques. Macaques live across Asia. The Japanese macaque, or snow monkey, lives in the snowy, mountainous parts of Japan. Other macaques, such as the stump-tailed macaque, live in **tropical** forests in southern Asia. There are also small groups of macaques called Barbary macaques that live in North Africa.

Barbary macaques live in the northern African countries of Algeria and Morocco and in Gibraltar, in southwestern Europe.

Rhesus monkeys are one of the most widespread and numerous of the macaques. Scientists have learned important things about how the human body works from studying the rhesus monkey. For example, before people were sent into space, scientists sent rhesus monkeys into space to study the effect that space travel had on their bodies.

The lion-tailed macaque lives in southern India.

These Japanese macaques are resting in a natural hot spring in Japan.

AN OLD WORLD MONKEY

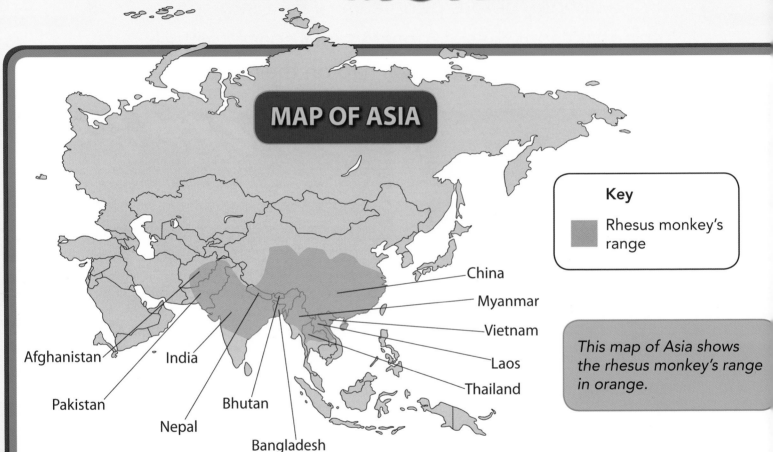

MAP OF ASIA

Key

Rhesus monkey's range

China

Myanmar

Vietnam

Laos

Thailand

Afghanistan

India

Pakistan

Bhutan

Nepal

Bangladesh

This map of Asia shows the rhesus monkey's range in orange.

Rhesus monkeys are called **Old World** monkeys. Old World monkeys are from Africa and Asia. Monkeys that live in Central America and South America are called **New World** monkeys. Old World monkeys have **opposable** thumbs for gripping things, which New World monkeys do not have.

Rhesus monkeys have light brown and gray hair. The hair on their heads is short. This helps show off their large ears and the expressions on their faces. Their faces and bottoms are hairless, and their skin is red. An adult monkey is about 2 feet (61 cm) tall, with a 1-foot-(30 cm) long tail.

One of the ways rhesus monkeys communicate is through the expressions on their face. Having a hairless face makes these expressions easier to see.

AN ADAPTABLE MONKEY

Rhesus monkeys have the biggest range of habitats of any primate, except for people. This rhesus monkey lives in a temple in Nepal.

Rhesus monkeys live in the Middle East and Asia, from Afghanistan to the eastern shores of China. You can find them in South Asia, in India, Bangladesh, and Nepal, and in Southeast Asia, too, in Bhutan, Myanmar, Laos, and Thailand.

Rhesus monkeys are very **adaptable**, meaning they can get used to different places and the problems they might find in them. They live in dry, hot deserts and in tropical rain forests. They live high in the Himalayas, where it is cold. They live on flat, grassy lands. They even live near humans. Rhesus monkeys have been found living in the crowded cities of northern India.

This rhesus monkey is climbing in a thick forest in India.

TIME TO EAT!

Rhesus monkeys are **omnivores**. This means they eat both plants and animals. They eat the roots, leaves, seeds, and fruit of plants. They also eat insects and small animals. Monkeys that live in places where the weather changes throughout the year often eat different foods in each season.

This rhesus monkey is eating a banana. When they live near people, these monkeys may take food from garbage cans and gardens.

As do many animals, rhesus monkeys play an important part in their **habitats**. The fruit they eat has seeds in it. These seeds pass through their bodies in the form of waste. Their waste puts the seeds back into the soil, where the seeds grow into new plants.

FUN FACT

Rhesus monkeys have special pouches, or pockets, in their cheeks. When food is easy to find, they store extra food in these pouches. When food is hard to find, they eat this stored food.

Rhesus monkeys' diets change depending on where the monkeys live and what is available there. This one is eating flowers.

LIVING TOGETHER

Rhesus monkeys live in groups, called troops. A troop is generally made up of a few males and many females that are closely related to one another. There are different rankings for males and females in a troop. Males are the **dominant** sex. Females lead the troop, though, because they form the heart of the group. Some troops have more than 200 members. When the troop's size reaches around 100 members, a subgroup of females may break off and start a new troop.

This troop of rhesus monkeys are resting together. Females generally stay with the troop they were born into for their whole lives. Males leave their birth troop when they reach adulthood.

Unlike most primates, rhesus monkeys do not fight over land. More than one troop might live in an area, but they hardly ever fight over the space.

MONKEYING AROUND

Rhesus monkeys most often swim to look for food, to play, or to cool off.

Rhesus monkeys are good climbers and swimmers. They spend most of their time on the ground, though. They are noisy, playful, and social. They talk to one another by making faces, moving their bodies in different ways, and making noises from their throats.

Rhesus monkeys communicate using sounds like barks, coos, and screams. They may also stare with their mouths open to threaten lower-ranking monkeys.

Rhesus monkeys are active during the day and sleep at night. Monkeys that live in forests, where food is easy to find, do not often go farther than 1 mile (2 km) from their sleeping nests. Rhesus monkeys that live in the mountains, where it is harder to find food, may travel up to 10 miles (16 km) from home to get food.

MALES AND FEMALES

Grooming is a way that rhesus monkeys bond with each other. Monkeys groom not only their mates, but also their offspring and other troop members.

Rhesus monkeys are adults and are old enough to **mate** when they are about four years old. When it is time to mate, a male rhesus monkey shows he is friendly to a female by carrying her young, **grooming** her fur, or bringing her food.

Rhesus monkeys that live where it is warm year-round may mate at different times throughout the year. Monkeys that live where winters are cold generally mate in the fall so that the babies will be born in the spring. Their babies are more likely to live if they are born when the weather is warm.

Male rhesus monkeys are larger and stronger than females. Female monkeys, like the one shown here, weigh about 10 pounds (4.5 kg), while male monkeys can weigh as much as 25 pounds (11 kg).

BABY MONKEYS

A baby monkey grows inside its mother for about five months. When it is born, it weighs just 1 pound (454 g). For the first weeks of its life, the baby will hold on to its mother's belly and travel with her wherever she goes. The father generally plays almost no part in raising the young.

Rhesus monkey mothers feed and groom their babies, as well as teach them the social rules of the troop.

As the baby rhesus monkey grows stronger, it will begin to ride on its mother's back. From this position, the baby can see and learn about the world around it. The baby monkey depends on its mother for milk for about a year. By this time, the mother may be ready to mate again.

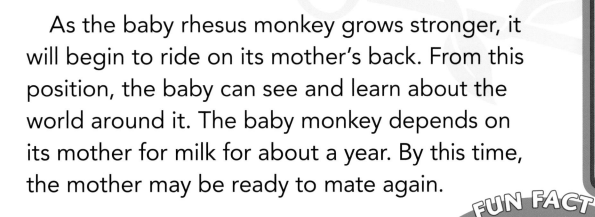

FUN FACT

In the wild, rhesus monkeys can live to be 30 years old. Monkeys that live in zoos can live as long as 35 years.

As baby rhesus monkeys get bigger, they leave their mothers' sides and make friends with other young troop members.

A PROBLEM FOR PEOPLE

In some places, rhesus monkeys live close to people. This can cause problems. Rhesus monkeys easily adapt to living near people. They often steal from crops and gardens. This makes them a pest to many people. Monkeys that live near people also tend to live shorter lives than monkeys living in the wild.

These rhesus monkeys are living in the city of New Delhi, India. Rhesus monkeys are sacred, or important, to people in India who follow the Hindu religion. Because of this, rhesus monkeys are allowed to roam freely in India's cities.

Poachers sometimes take rhesus monkeys from the wild. This can upset the balance of males and females in a troop and lead to a drop in rhesus monkey numbers. People have started setting aside places where rhesus monkeys can live in their natural habitat. This will help keep them safe and healthy for years to come.

Glossary

adaptable (uh-DAPT-uh-bel) Able to change to fit new conditions.

dominant (DAH-mih-nent) Strongest.

grooming (GROOM-ing) Cleaning the body and making it appear neat.

habitats (HA-buh-tats) The surroundings where animals or plants naturally live.

mate (MAYT) To come together to make babies.

New World (NOO WURLD) North America and South America.

Old World (OHLD WURLD) The part of the world that includes Asia, Africa, and Europe.

omnivores (OM-nih-vawrz) Animals that eat both plants and animals.

opposable (uh-POH-zuh-bel) Able to hold digits on a hand or foot together.

poachers (POH-cherz) People who illegally take animals that are protected by the law out of the wild.

primates (PRY-mayts) The group of animals that are more advanced than others and includes monkeys, gorillas, and people.

social (SOH-shul) Living together in a group.

species (SPEE-sheez) One kind of living thing. All people are one species.

tropical (TRAH-puh-kul) Having to do with the warm parts of Earth that are near the equator.

Index

A
adults, 18
Asia, 6, 8, 10

B
body, 7, 13, 16

C
Central America, 8

D
discoveries, 5

F
forests, 6, 11, 17

G
group(s), 4, 6, 14

H
humans, 5, 11. *See also* people

J
Japan, 6

M
macaques, 4, 6–7
males, 14, 22
medicine, 5
Middle East, 10

N
North Africa, 6

O
omnivores, 12

P
people, 5, 7, 22. *See also* humans
plants, 12–13
poachers, 22
primates, 5, 15
problems, 11, 22

S
science, 5
scientists, 7
seeds, 12–13
skin, 9
space, 7
species, 4, 6

T
thumbs, 8

Web Sites

Due to the changing nature of Internet links, PowerKids Press has developed an online list of Web sites related to the subject of this book. This site is updated regularly. Please use this link to access the list: www.powerkidslinks.com/monk/rhesus/